Securing the Home Front:
A Practical Guide To Surviving Military Deployment

By Karen J. Clinton

I0541800

Securing the Home Front: A Practical
Guide To Surviving Military Deployment

Written by Karen J. Clinton

ISBN: 979-8-9864810-9-8

Wade Christian Publishing LLC
www.wadepublishers.com
info@wadepublishers.com

Securing the Home Front

Synopsis

In this essential guide, you'll find:

- **Emotional Support Strategies:** Learn how to manage the rollercoaster of emotions and maintain your mental well-being.

- **Communication Tips:** Discover practical ways to stay connected with your deployed loved one despite the distance.

- **Practical Advice:** Get organized with tips on handling finances, household responsibilities, and childcare.

- **Community Resources:** Explore available support networks and how to tap into them for assistance.

Introduction

*L*ife is going well until suddenly, the white paper or email with what seems like the tiniest writing is received. It's the dreaded Military Orders. The truth is, you knew this day would come. You just hoped by some divine intervention that your loved one's number would never be called. You didn't think it would happen so soon, or maybe you delayed preparation because the stress of it all made you procrastinate. Yes, people procrastinate because they are stressed, not because they are lazy or unmotivated. Whatever you are feeling, this is not the time to give up, quit, throw in the towel, cave in, or fall into depression. You must put action steps in place, handle business, and *secure the home*

front. Your marriage, your mental stability, and your family depend on YOU.

If you're new to life in the military, you will encounter a lot of jargon. The Home Front is associated with deployment. Merriam-Webster defines it as "the people who stay in a country and work while that country's soldiers are fighting a war in a foreign country." The spouse or family member back at home is often said to be at the Home Front.

While deployment can be very stressful, there are no surprises here, right? You supported your loved one who enlisted or said, "I DO!"

Now that reality has set in, let me share with you a few practical tips that will lessen the blow of your soldier involuntarily leaving the family for months to a year at a time and will aid your temporary transition into life without their day-to-day presence.

Tip 1
Find Out About the Soldier and Family Readiness Group (SFRG) and Stay Connected

Soldiers must have positive and understanding support at home. During soldiers' deployment, their unit develops an organized, reliable support network where spouses and family members can turn for information, including, "What time are flights leaving? Where are farewell ceremonies held? Where do we mail care packages, etc?"

The Soldier and Family Readiness Group (SFRG) is a support network for military families. It provides them with resources, information, and a sense of community during deployments and other military-related events. Staying connected to the SFRG is vital for several reasons:

• **You will have direct access to information:** The SFRG provides essential information about deployment schedules, family support resources, and status updates on the military member. This information can be critical in helping family members stay informed and prepared during a deployment. Don't rely on your soldier for the small details during this time. Some things about the mission cannot be shared with spouses and family. Try not to be offended or take this personally.

• **You will receive emotional support:** The SFRG provides emotional support to military families by connecting them with other families going through similar experiences. This sense of community can help families feel less isolated and more supported during a deployment.

• **You will have access to resources:**
The SFRG can expose families to resources such as counseling services and financial and employment assistance. These resources can be critical in helping families manage the challenges of deployment.

• **You will stay informed:**
The SFRG provides families opportunities to stay updated on the military member's unit and its activities. This can help families feel more connected to their loved one's service and alleviate some of the stress and anxiety that may come with separation. Some SFRGs have private Facebook groups where photos of training exercises are shared, questions are answered, and you can share and receive

encouragement from interaction with others. During my son's first deployment, I linked up with his unit's SFRG through Facebook. I felt relieved to see photos of my son. It meant the world to me to receive first-hand information about welcome home ceremonies, promotions, and awards.

Affiliation with the SFRG helps military families feel supported and informed during deployments and other military-related events.

Tip 2
SEND CARE PACKAGES AND LETTERS OFTEN
(Share video updates of family and children's milestones)

Technology has increased so much since my husband's deployment in 2007 during the Afghanistan War and Securing Iraqi Freedom. Back then, we didn't have phones with video capabilities. International charges were astronomical for cell phone conversations, and we didn't have access to free services like Messenger Calls or Google Voice. My husband and I racked up $700 - $800 in phone bills monthly for the 10-minute calls 1-2 times per week if my husband's schedule allowed. I sent letters with care packages weekly and mailed separate letters every three days. You can never run out of things to write about. It's imperative to send encouraging notes, scriptures, or words of affirmation, telling your soldier how proud you are of them for defending our freedom. If you have children, let them send letters or drawings. Receiving mail will make your soldier feel appreciated and more connected to home.

Some deployments are different. Your soldier may be far from combat or on classified missions with limited to no contact with civilians. Although you may be able to talk with them regularly or use video calling, you should still prioritize sending care packages with their favorite snack, toiletry items, etc.

Tip 3
Know the American Red Cross
Emergency Contact Number

Many things can happen during deployment. Emergency communication messages are the heart of what the Red Cross does to help military families during difficult times. The American Red Cross supports families through the Hero Care Center. In times of emergency and major life events, such as births, deaths, and family fires, the Red Cross helps military families communicate with their loved ones. The Hero Care Network is available online, by phone, and through the mobile app, 24 hours a day, 7 days a week.

U.S. military service members and their families can initiate a request for Red Cross emergency assistance and track its progress from anywhere in the world. Here are four ways to reach the Center: (1) **submit a request online at** redcross.org, (2) download the free Hero Care app, (3) Text 'GETHEROCARE' to 90999, or (4) call the Red Cross at 1-877-272-7337.

Before connecting with the American Red Cross, it is helpful to have the following information ready:

- Service member's full legal name
- Service member's rank/rating
- Branch of service (Army, Navy, Air Force, Marines, Coast Guard)
- Last 4 digits of the service member's social security number or date of birth
- Military unit address
- Military Installation
- Rear detachment (if applicable)

It is also helpful to have as much information about the emergency as possible. Including the following:

- Name and complete contact information for the immediate family member experiencing the emergency (could be spouse, parent, child/grandchild, or grandparent)
- Nature of the emergency (city, state)
- Where the emergency took place

The American Red Cross emergency service was beneficial to me when my stepfather passed away. My husband was able to leave deployment and return home for the funeral. My son was able to do the same when my biological father passed away just before the COVID-19 pandemic forced our country to shut down.

Tip 4
Take Care of Home
(Declutter to eliminate
unnecessary stress, frustration,
and safety hazards)

Deployments are inherently stressful. A decluttered, clean, and organized home environment helps reduce additional stress for some people. A cluttered living or working space can create a sense of chaos, leading to stress, anxiety, and being overwhelmed. Removing unnecessary items and organizing your space can create a sense of calm and order, which can positively affect your mental state.

In addition to reducing stress, decluttering can also have other benefits, such as increased productivity, improved focus, and greater control over your environment. Keeping up with household chores helps maintain normalcy and routine. Knowing that things are being taken care of at home can help the deployed spouse focus on their duties without worrying about domestic issues. Remaining consistent with regular chores like cleaning, taking out the trash, and maintaining the yard is essential for health and safety. However, neglecting these can lead to health hazards or even safety risks. For families with children, continuing to do chores sets an excellent example of responsibility and resilience. It can help children cope better with the absence of their deployed parent. Moreover, when the deployed soldier returns, having a well-maintained home can ease the integration process and make the transition smoother for everyone involved.

However, it's important to note that decluttering is not a one-time solution to stress. Clutter can quickly build up over time, so it's crucial to declutter and organize regularly to maintain calm and order in your space. Consider hiring a cleaning service to help maintain the home if your finances allow. There is no shame in needing help. During the busy season in my life, we utilized cleaning and laundry wash/fold services biweekly. That was a game-changer.

Tip 5
Keep Busy and Find a Second Support System (There's no time for depression)

Keeping busy is important for family members of deployed soldiers. Being occupied with meaningful activities and responsibilities can help manage worries and anxieties. It provides a healthy distraction and prevents excessive rumination on the uncertainties and risks associated with deployment. Engaging in significant activities can give family members a sense of purpose and accomplishment during deployment, whether pursuing personal interests, focusing on career goals, or volunteering in the community.

Avoiding idleness helps with productivity and fulfillment. Deployment can disrupt the regular routine of daily life for military families; taking on selective projects or other activities contributes to developing resilience. By facing challenges head-on and being proactive, families learn to adapt to new situations and overcome obstacles, which helps them cope with the demands of deployment more effectively. Ensure you deliberately include a self-care routine such as exercising, relaxation techniques, or creative outlets (painting, pottery, etc.). Taking care of yourself mentally, emotionally, and spiritually is essential for maintaining balance and coping with the stress of deployment.

When my husband deployed, I was in school, working on obtaining my bachelor's degree. I was working a full-time job as well. I decided to take control of my health by joining a women's fitness center. My routine consisted of dropping my children off at school in the morning, going to the gym to work out, showering, then heading to work for eight hours, going to class, picking the kids up, and going home. I went to class four days a week and on Saturday mornings. My mother was my support system in keeping the kids while I was in class during the week and on some Saturdays. Having a support system is vital. I purposely kept busy. I rationalized that it made the deployment time go by quicker. Fast forward, I graduated magna cum laude with a bachelor's degree in Sociology. This accomplishment was significant because I became the first college graduate among my ten siblings. To top it off, my husband was able to attend my graduation because he was on block leave.

Keeping busy, focusing, and utilizing your support system produces great dividends during deployment.

Tip 6
Ensure Bills are Paid
and Finances are Intact

Preparing financially before deployment is crucial to ensure a family's stability and well-being during separation. There's nothing like peace of mind knowing the Home Front isn't struggling due to money issues. Here are some steps a deploying soldier can take to prepare.

- **Create a Spending Plan**
  Develop a detailed spending plan or "budget" outlining all expenses and income. Budget can seem like a curse word, but it will outline the family's financial situation and aid in determining where adjustments can be made if necessary.

- **Set up an Emergency Fund**
  Establish an emergency fund before deployment, if at all possible, to cover unexpected expenses such as medical emergencies or car repairs. Aim to have at least three to six months of living expenses saved up. Use these funds for genuine emergencies only. Doing so requires discipline, but you have what it takes!

- **Review Financial Obligations and Reduce Expenses**
  Ensure all bills, loans, and other financial obligations are current. If money isn't tight, consider setting up automatic payments to avoid missed payments and automatic transfers for savings and investments while

deployed. If money is tight, look for ways to reduce expenses. Cancel or suspend non-essential services such as gym memberships, TV subscriptions, or cable. The soldier may be able to downgrade vehicle insurance policies to a car in-storage policy if no one will drive it while deployed. This can be quickly reversed when the soldier returns home or if the vehicle is needed. Adding one's spouse or a trusted individual as an authorized contact person with creditors will make handling business in the soldier's absence easier.

- **Power of Attorney**
  Grant your spouse, a trusted family member, or a friend power of

attorney to handle financial matters in your absence. This allows them to manage finances, sign documents, and make financial decisions on your behalf, so having a "trusted" person is essential. The creation of the Power of Attorney is a free service offered through the U.S. Armed Forces Legal Assistance Office. You can find an office near you by going to https://legalassistance.law.af.mil

- **Life Insurances and Wills**
  Review and update life insurance policies and create or update all wills. Ensure trusted beneficiaries are correctly listed and that your family will be taken care of financially in the event of the worst-case scenario.

- **Utilize Military Resources**
  The military provides financial resources, such as financial counseling, budgeting workshops, and deployment assistance programs. These resources can provide valuable guidance and support.

- **Communication**
  Maintain open communication with your family about financial matters. Discuss budgeting strategies, financial goals, and how to handle any unexpected expenses that may arise.

By taking these proactive steps, a deploying soldier can help ensure their family is financially prepared and supported during their absence.

Tip 7
Stay Mentally Strong
through Prayer

Prayer, meditation, and mental strength play significant roles in supporting spouses or loved ones of deployed soldiers for several reasons:

- **Emotional Support**
  Prayer provides spouses and loved ones comfort and peace during times of uncertainty and stress. It serves as a solace, allowing them to express their fears, hopes, and concerns to a higher power.

- **Coping Mechanism**
  Maintaining mental strength is crucial for spouses facing deployment challenges. Prayer and meditation can help them cope with the emotional rollercoaster of separation, loneliness, and worry by providing inner strength and resilience.

- **Sense of Connection**
  Prayer fosters a sense of spiritual connection with God and our loved ones, even when physically apart. It allows families to rely on a source outside of ourselves and activates safety and protection for our loved ones.

- **Finding Purpose and Meaning**
  Engaging in prayer and maintaining

mental strength can help families discover purpose and meaning during deployment. It can serve as a reminder of the importance of their role in supporting their family.

- **Positive Outlook**
Prayer and mental strength can help families maintain a positive outlook, focusing on gratitude, hope, and faith rather than dwelling on negative emotions such as fear, worry, and anxiety.

- **Resilience Building**
Cultivating mental strength through prayer and meditation can help families develop resilience, allowing them to navigate the ups and downs

of deployment effectively and bounce back from setbacks.

- **Community Support**
  Engaging in prayer and spiritual practices often involves participation in supportive communities such as church attendance, other religious groups, or prayer circles. These communities can provide additional sources of emotional support and understanding for spouses and family members of deployed soldiers.

Overall, prayer and mental strength are essential tools for spouses and families of deployed soldiers to navigate the challenges of separation, uncertainty, and stress while fostering resilience, hope, and connection during this difficult time.

Final Thoughts and Practical Tips

As we conclude this journey together, let's take a moment to reflect on the key points we've discussed. Preparing for deployment is a multifaceted process that involves careful planning, strong support networks, and a focus on emotional well-being.

- **Create a Deployment Plan**
  Ensure you have a detailed plan covering all deployment aspects, from finances to daily routines.

- **Establish and Maintain Support Networks**
  Connect with family, friends, and social groups with similar values to build a robust support system.

- **Set Up Communication Methods**
  When possible, use technology to stay in touch and set realistic expectations for communication frequency. Remember that your deployed loved one may have limited communications due to a physical location or OPSEC (Operations Security).

- **Organize Important Documents**
  Keep all critical documents organized and accessible. (Birth Certificates, Marriage Licenses, POAs, Wills, Deeds, Medical Records, Passwords, Insurance Documents, Real Estate and Car Titles.)

- **Prepare for Emergencies**
  Have an emergency plan ready, including key contacts and procedures. Establish a family meeting point. Non-perishable food items, weather radios, water, blankets, batteries, first aid kits, and fire blankets are essentials for your preparedness kit.

- **Personal Stories**
  Draw inspiration from military spouses and other family members who have successfully navigated deployments. Their experiences remind us that while deployment is challenging, it is also a time of growth, adjustment, and alignment.

Emotional Preparedness

Deployment can be an emotional rollercoaster. It's essential to acknowledge your feelings and seek support when needed—practice self-care by engaging in activities that bring you joy and relaxation. Capture your feelings by journaling. Keep your journal and review your emotional growth. You may see areas that still need improvement, but you'll be surprised at how much you've grown. If you have children, maintain routines and provide them with extra emotional support. Be sensitive to changes in a child's behavior and recognize when one-on-one time is needed.

Encouragement and Positivity

Remember, you are stronger than you think. Stay positive and look for opportunities for growth during this challenging time. While the distance can feel daunting, each day brings you closer to reunification. Focus on your strengths, your family's flexibility, the love and support that binds you, and celebrate small victories. Surround yourself with supportive friends and community. Find joy in activities that uplift your spirits. Your courage in this journey is inspiring. Remain hopeful, and know that brighter days are ahead.

Prayer of Encouragement

I want to end this guide with a prayer for you and your family:

Heavenly Father,
We come before You with hearts full of gratitude and concern as we lift this soldier preparing to deploy. We thank You for the strength, courage, and commitment You've given them, and we pray for Your protection to surround them like a shield in every moment of the journey.

Give them wisdom in every decision, calm during challenges, and faith that can move mountains. Let them feel Your presence, knowing that You are with them every step of the way, guarding and guiding them.

Father, we also pray for their family during this time of separation. Grant them comfort and reassurance that You are watching over their soldier. Fill their hearts with peace that surpasses understanding and the strength to endure each day apart. Surround them with a community of support and love so they never feel alone.

Help them trust Your plan, knowing that You control every detail. May this deployment time strengthen their bond and deepen their reliance on You. Protect their hearts from fear and anxiety, and replace it with faith and hope in Your promises.

I place this soldier and their family into Your loving hands, confident that You will watch over them and bring them back together safely. In the holy name of Jesus, we pray.

Amen.

Closing Remarks

Remember, you are not alone on this journey. Speak with other families, engage, and reach out. With preparation, support, and a positive outlook, you and your family will emerge stronger. Stay resilient, stay connected, and know that you have the strength to overcome any challenge.

Thank you for your dedication and service.

Resources

Here are some organizations and resources that offer support to military families:

- Military OneSource - a web-based resource provided by the Department of Defense: https://www.militaryonesource.mil

- The American Red Cross - https://www.redcross.org

- Sesame Workshop for Military Families - https://seasameworkshop.org

- United Through Reading - https://unitedthroughreading.org

Author Karen J. Clinton is a graduate of Claflin University with a Bachelor of Arts Degree and a Master of Business Administration from Southern Wesleyan University.

She is married to Trevor Clinton, a 21-year Army veteran. They have three children, one of whom is currently a soldier, and two grandchildren.

Karen and her family are deeply rooted in their faith. They are help ministers at Right Direction Church International in Columbia, SC, under the leadership of Bishop Herbert and Dr. Marcia Bailey.